The New Mixed Drinks Collection
Shooters

R&R PUBLICATIONS MARKETING PTY LTD

This edition published in 1999 by
R&R Publications Marketing Pty. Ltd.
(ACN 083 612 579)
12 Edward Street, Brunswick, Victoria. 3056
Australia wide Toll Free: 1 800 063 296

Publisher: Richard Carroll
Mixed Drinks Research: Marc Phillips & Jon Carroll
Original Design: Sean McNamara
Data Entry: Jenny Ring
Cover Design: Carlton Studios
Photography: Warren Webb
Presentation: Anthony Carroll
Photography Assistance: Samantha Carroll

ISBN: 1-74022-026-9

Printed August 1999

Scanning by: PICA Overseas Ltd, Singapore
Computer Typeset in ITC Eras and Palatino
Printed by: APP, Singapore

Acknowledgements

The publishers wish to thank and acknowledge the following companies
and individuals, without whose help and assistance this book would not
have been possible.
Special thanks to Juliana Nguyen, Brand Manager of Seagram Australia Pty.
Ltd. for her assistance and advice in the development of this book.

Phillip Lazarus – Australian Agent for Libbey Glass of America
Cnr. Beauchamp Rd. and McPherson St., Matraville NSW 2036
Suppliers of: A wide range of quality glassware to the retail and hospitality trade.

ACI Crown Glassware Ltd.
816 Bourke St., Waterloo NSW 2017
Suppliers of: A diverse range of glassware especially designed for the
hospitality industry.

Alpen Products Pty. Ltd.
130 Old Pittwater Rd., Brookvale NSW 2100
Suppliers of: Party novelties, decorations, toothpicks, swizzle sticks and
other drink and party accessories.

Remy Australie
484 Victoria Rd., Gladesville NSW 2111
Suppliers of: Galliano, Amaretto di Galliano, Sambuca di Galliano, Lago
Nera Galliano, Cointreau and many other fine wines and spirits.

Seagram Australia Pty. Limited
32 Jasmine Street, Botany, NSW 2019
Suppliers of: Seagram's Liqueurs, ABSOLUT VODKA, ABSOLUT CITRON,
ABSOLUT KURANT, Chivas Regal Scotch Whisky, Royal Salute Scotch Whisky,
The Black Douglas Scotch Whisky, 100 Pipers Scotch Whisky, Heritage
Selection Scotch Whisky: Longmorn, Strathisla, Benriach, Glen Keith, The
Glenlivet Scotch Whisky, Cougar Bourbon, Chatelle Napoleon Brandy,
Martell Cognac, Captain Morgan Rum, Karloff Vodka, Coyote Tequila,
Akropolis Oyzo, Seagram's London Dry Gin, Lochan Ora Liqueur, Sabra
Chocolate Orange Liqueur, Mumm Champagne.

Cadbury-Schweppes Pty. Ltd.
636 St Kilda Rd., Melbourne Victoria 3000
Suppliers of: Drink mixers, including Bitter Lemon, Dry Ginger Ale, Soda
Water, Tonic Water, Lemonade, Lemon, Lime, Bitters & Soda.

Table of Contents

METHODS OF MIXING COCKTAILS

The four methods below are the most common processes of mixing cocktails:-

1. Shake   **2.** Stir
3. Build   **4.** Blend

1. SHAKE: To shake is to mix a cocktail by shaking it in a cocktail shaker by hand. First, fill the glass part of the shaker three quarters full with ice, then pour the ingredients on top of the ice. Less expensive ingredients are more frequently poured before the deluxe ingredients. Pour the contents of the glass into the metal part of the shaker and shake vigorously for ten to fifteen seconds. Remove the glass section and using a Hawthorn strainer, strain contents into the cocktail glass.

Shaking ingredients that do not mix easily with spirits is easy and practical (juices, egg whites, cream and sugar syrups).

Most shakers have two or three parts. In a busy bar, the cap is often temporarily misplaced. If this happens, a coaster or the inside palm of your hand is quite effective. American shakers are best.

To sample the cocktail before serving to the customer, pour a small amount into the shaker cap and using a straw check the taste.

2. STIR: To stir a cocktail is to mix the ingredients by stirring them with ice in a mixing glass and then straining them into a chilled cocktail glass. Short circular twirls are most preferred. (NB. The glass part of the American shaker will do well for this.) Spirits, liqueurs and vermouths that blend easily together are mixed by this method.

3. BUILD: To build a cocktail is to mix the ingredients in the glass in which the cocktail is to be served, floating one on top of the other.

Hi-Ball, long fruit juice and carbonated mixed cocktails are typically built using this technique. Where possible a swizzle stick should be put into the drink to mix the ingredients after being presented to the customer. Long straws are excellent substitutes when swizzle sticks are unavailable.

4. BLEND: To blend a cocktail is to mix the ingredients using an electric blender/mixer. It is recommended to add the fruit (fresh or tinned) first. Slicing small pieces gives a smoother texture than if you add the whole fruit. Next, pour the alcohol. Ice should always be added last. This order ensures that the fruit is blended freely with the alcoholic ingredients allowing the ice to gradually mix into the food and beverage, chilling the flavour. Ideally, the blender should be on for at least 20 seconds. Following this procedure will prevent ice and fruit lumps that then need to be strained.

If the blender starts to rattle and hum, ice may be obstructing the blades from spinning. Always check that the blender is clean before you start. Angostura Bitters is ammonia based which is suitable for cleaning. Fill 4 to 5 shakes with hot water, rinse and then wipe clean.

TECHNIQUES IN MAKING COCKTAILS

1. SHAKE AND POUR: After shaking the cocktail, pour the contents straight into the glass. When pouring into Hi-Ball glasses and sometimes old fashioned glasses the ice cubes are included. This eliminates straining.

2. SHAKE AND STRAIN: Using a Hawthorn strainer (or knife) this technique prevents the ice going into the glass. Straining protects the cocktail ensuring melted ice won't dilute the flavour and mixture.

3. FLOAT INGREDIENTS: Hold the spoon right way up and rest it with the lip slightly above the level of the last layer. Fill spoon gently and the contents will flow smoothly from all around the rim. Use the back of the spoons dish only if you are experienced.

4. FROSTING (sugar and salt rims): This technique is used to coat the rim of the glass with either salt or sugar. First, rub lemon/orange slice juice all the way around only the glass rim. Next, holding the glass by the stem upside down, rest on a plate containing salt or sugar and turn slightly so that it adheres to the glass. Pressing the glass too deeply into the salt or sugar often results in chunks sticking to the glass. A lemon slice is used for salt and an orange slice is used for sugar.

To achieve colour affects, put a small amount of grenadine or coloured liqueur in a plate and coat the rim of the glass, then gently place it in the sugar. The grenadine absorbs the sugar and turns it pink. This is much easier than mixing grenadine with sugar and then trying to get it to stick to the glass.

HELPFUL HINTS

Cocktail mixing is an art which is expressed in the preparation and presentation of the cocktail.

HOW TO MAKE A BRANDY ALEXANDER CROSS

Take two short straws and, with a sharp knife, slice one of the straws half way through in the middle and wedge the other uncut straw into the cut straw to create a cross.

STORING FRUIT JUICES

Take a 750ml bottle and soak it in hot water to remove the label and sterilise the alcohol. The glass has excellent appeal and you'll find it easier to pour the correct measurement with an attached nip pourer.

SUGAR SYRUP RECIPE

Fill a cup or bowl (depending on how much you want to make) with white sugar, top it up with boiling water until the receptacle is just about full and keep stirring until the sugar is fully dissolved. Refrigerate when not in use. Putting a teaspoon of sugar into a cocktail is being lazy, it does not do the job properly as the sugar dissolves.

JUICE TIPS

Never leave juices, Coconut Cream or other ingredients in cans. Pour them into clean bottles, cap and refrigerate them. All recipes in this book have been tested with Berri fruit juices.

ICE

Ice is probably the most important part of cocktails. It is used in nearly all cocktails. Consequently ice must be clean and fresh at all times.

The small squared cubes and flat chips of ice are superior for chilling and mixing cocktails. Ice cubes with holes are inefficient. Wet ice, ice scraps and broken ice should only be used in blenders.

CRUSHED ICE

Take the required amount of ice and fold into a clean linen cloth. Although uncivilised, the most effective method is to smash it against the bar floor. Shattering with a bottle may break the bottle. Certain retailers sell portable ice crushers. Alternatively a blender may be used. Half fill with ice and then pour water into the blender until it reaches the level of the ice. Blend for about 30 seconds, strain out the water and you have perfectly crushed ice. Always try and use a metal scoop to collect the ice from the ice tray.

Never pick up the ice with your hands. This is unhygienic. Shovelling the glass into the ice tray to gather ice can also cause breakages and hence should be avoided where possible.

It is important that the ice tray is cleaned each day. As ice is colourless and odourless, many people assume wrongly it is always clean. Taking a cloth soaked in hot water, wipe the inside of the bucket warm. The blenders used for all of our bar requirements are Moulinex blenders with glass bowls. We have found these blenders to be of exceptional quality.

GLASSES

Cordial (Embassy):	30ml	Fancy Hi-Ball Glass:	220ml, 350ml, 470ml
Cordial (Lexington):	37ml	Hurricane Glass:	230ml, 440ml, 650ml
Tall Dutch Cordial:	45ml	Irish Coffee Glass:	250ml
Whisky Shot:	45ml	Margarita Glass:	260ml
Martini Glass:	90ml	Hi-Ball Glass:	270ml, 285ml, 330ml
Cocktail Glass:	90ml, 140ml	Footed Hi-Ball Glass:	270ml, 300ml
Champagne Saucer:	140ml	Salud Grande Glass:	290ml
Champagne Flute:	140ml, 180ml	Fiesta Grande Glass:	350ml, 490ml
Wine Goblet:	140ml, 190ml	Poco Grande Glass:	380ml
Old Fashioned Spirit:	185ml, 210ml, 290ml	Brandy Balloon:	650ml
Fancy Cocktail:	210ml, 300ml		

A proven method to cleaning glasses is to hold each glass individually over a bucket of boiling water until the glass becomes steamy and then with a clean linen cloth rub in a circular way to ensure the glass is polished for the next serve

Cocktails can be poured into any glass but the better the glass the better the appearance of the cocktail.

One basic rule should apply and that is, use no coloured glasses as they spoil the appearance of cocktails. All glasses have been designed for a specific task, e.g.,

1. Hi-Ball glasses for long cool refreshing drinks.
2. Cocktail glasses for short sharp, or stronger drinks.
3. Champagne saucers for creamy after-dinner style drinks, etc.,

The stem of the glass has been designed so you may hold it whilst polishing, leaving the bowl free of marks and germs so that you may enjoy your drink. All cocktail glasses should be kept in a refrigerator or filled with ice while you are preparing the cocktails in order to chill the glass. An appealing affect on a 90ml cocktail glass can be achieved by running the glass under cold water and then placing it in the freezer.

GARNISHES AND JUICES

Banana	Onions
Celery	Oranges
Cucumber	Pineapple
Lemons	Red Maraschino Cherries
Limes	Rockmelon
Mint leaves	Strawberries
Olives	Canned fruit
Celery salt	Nutmeg
Chocolate flake	Pepper, Salt
Cinnamon	Tomato
Fresh eggs	Sugar and sugar cubes
Fresh single cream	Tabasco sauce
Fresh milk	Worcestershire sauce
Apple	Orange and Mango
Carbonated waters	Pineapple
Coconut Cream	Sugar syrup
Lemon – pure	Canned nectars
Orange	Canned pulps
Jelly Babies	Crushed Pineapple
Almonds	Blueberries
Apricot Conserve	Red Cocktail Onions
Vanilla Ice Cream	Flowers (assorted)

Simplicity is the most important fact to keep in mind when garnishing cocktails. Do not overdo the garnish; make it striking, but if you can't get near the cocktail to drink it then you have failed. Most world champion cocktails just have a lemon slice, or a single red cherry.

Tall refreshing Hi-Balls tend to have more garnish as the glass is larger. A swizzle stick should be served nearly always in long cocktails. Straws are always served for a lady, but optional for a man.

Plastic animals, umbrellas, fans and a whole variety of novelty goods are available to garnish, and they add a lot of fun to the drink.

ALCOHOL RECOMMENDED FOR A COCKTAIL BAR
Spirits

Bourbon – Cougar	Rum – Captain Morgan
Brandy – Chatelle Napoleon	Schnapps
Campari	Scotch – Chivas Regal
Canadian Club	Scotch – The Black Douglas
Gin – Seagram's London Dry	Scotch – The Glenlivet
Malibu	Southern Comfort
Ouzo – Akropolis	Tennessee Whiskey – Jack Daniel's
Pernod	Tequila – Coyote
Pernod	Vodka – ABSOLUT VODKA
Rum – Bacardi	

Liqueurs

Advocaat	Frangelico
Amaretto di Saronno	Galliano
Bailey's Irish Cream	Grand Marnier
Benedictine	Kahlúa
Blue Curacao	Kirsch
Cassis	Banana
Chartreuse – Green & Yellow	Mango
Cherry Advocaat	Melon
Cherry Brandy	Orange
Clayton's Tonic (Non-alcoholic)	Peach
Coconut	Pimm's
Cointreau	Sambuca – Clear
Creme de Cafe	Sambuca – Black
Creme de Menthe Green	Strawberry
Dark Creme de Cacao	Tia Maria
Drambuie	Triple Sec

Vermouth

Cinzano Bianco Vermouth	Martini Bianco Vermouth
Cinzano Dry Vermouth	Martini Dry Vermouth
Cinzano Rosso Vermouth	Martini Rosso Vermouth

ESSENTIAL EQUIPMENT FOR A COCKTAIL BAR

Cocktail shaker	Waiter's friend corkscrew
Hawthorn Strainer	Bottle openers
Mixing glass	Ice scoop
Spoon with muddler	Ice bucket
Moulinex Electric blender	Free pourers
Knife, cutting board	Swizzle sticks, straws
Measures (jiggers)	Coasters and napkins
Can opener	Scooper spoon (long teaspoon)
Hand cloths for cleaning glasses	

DESCRIPTION OF LIQUEURS AND SPIRITS

Advocaat: A combination of fresh egg yolks, sugar, brandy, vanilla and spirit. Limited shelf life, Recommend shelf life 12-15 months from manufacture.

Amaretto: A rich subtle liqueur with a unique almond flavour.

Angostura Bitters: An essential part of any bar or kitchen. A unique additive whose origins date back to 1824. A mysterious blend of natural herbs and spices, both a seasoning and flavouring agent, in both sweet and savoury dishes and drinks. Ideal for dieters as it is low in sodium and calories.

Baileys Irish Cream: The largest selling liqueur in the world, was introduced onto the Australian market in 1974. It is a blend of Irish Whiskey, softened by Irish Cream and other flavourings. It is a natural product.

Benedictine: A perfect end to a perfect meal. Serve straight, with ice, soda, or as part of a favourite cocktail.

Bourbon – Cougar: Has the smooth, deep, easy flavour consistent with an authentic premium bourbon whiskey.

Brandy – Chatelle Napoleon: 100 per cent French Brandy, light amber in colour, fruity with light oak aromas and a long aftertaste. Ideal neat or great for mixing.

Campari: A drink for many occasions, both as a long or short drink, or as a key ingredient in many fashionable cocktails.

Cassis: Deep, rich purple promises and delivers a blackcurrant flavour and aroma. Cassis lends itself to neat drinking or an endless array of delicious sauces and desserts.

Chartreuse: A liqueur available in either yellow or green colour. Made by the monks of the Carthusian order. The only world famous liqueur still made by monks.

Cherry Advocaat: Same as Advocaat, plus natural cherry flavours and colour is added.

Cherry Brandy: Is made from concentrated, morello cherry juice. Small quantity of bitter almonds and vanilla is added to make it more enjoyable as a neat drink before or after dinner. Excellent for mixers, topping, ice cream, fruit salads, pancakes, etc.

Coconut: A smooth liqueur, composed of exotic coconut, heightened with light-bodied white rum.

Cointreau: Made from a neutral grain spirit, as opposed to Cognac. An aromatic flavour of natural citrus fruits.

Creme de Cacao Dark: Rich, deep chocolate. Smooth and classy. Serve on its own, or mix for all kinds of delectable treats.

Creme de Cacao White: This liqueur delivers a light chocolate flavour. Excellent ingredient when absence of colour is desired.

Creme de Grand Marnier: A blend of Grand Marnier and smooth French cream. A premium product, a very smooth taste with the orange/cognac flavour blending beautifully with smooth cream. Introduced to Australia in 1985.

Creme de Menthe Green: Clear peppermint flavour, reminiscent of a fresh, crisp, clean winter's day in the mountains. Excellent mixer, a necessity in the gourmet kitchen.

Creme de Menthe White: As Creme de Menthe Green, when colour is not desired.

Curacao Blue: A combination of citrus flavours with brilliant blue colour to make some cocktails more exciting.

Curacao Orange: Citrus flavour with orange colouring, used for a variety of cocktail mixers.

Curacao Triple Sec: Based on natural citrus fruits. Well known fact is citrus fruits are the most important aromatic flavour constituents. Interesting to know citrus fruit was known 2,000 years before Christ. As a liqueur one of the most versatile. Can be enjoyed with or without ice as a neat drink, or used in mixed cocktails more than any other liqueur. Triple Sec – also known as White Curacao or Curacao.

Galliano: The distinguished taste! A classic liqueur that blends with a vast array of mixed drinks.

Gin – Seagram's London Dry: Extra dry because of Seagram's original mellowing process. Its aroma comes from using the highest quality juniper berries; it is smooth, crystal clear, refreshing and very dry. The perfect mixer for both short and long drinks.

Kirsch: A fruit brandy distilled from morello cherries. Used to enhance the flavour of fruit.

Drambuie: A Scotch whisky liqueur. Made from a secret recipe dating back to 1745. "Dram Buidheach" the drink that satisfies.

Frangelico: A precious liqueur imported from Italy. Made from wild hazelnuts with infusions of berries and flowers to enrich the flavour.

Grand Marnier: An original blend of fine old Cognac and an extract of oranges. The recipe is over 150 years old

Kahlúa: A smooth, dark liqueur made from real coffee and fine clear spirits. Its origins are based in Mexico.

Banana: Fresh ripe bananas are the perfect base for the definitive daiquiri and a host of other exciting fruit cocktails.

Malibu: A clear liqueur based on white rum with the subtle addition of coconut. Its distinctive taste blends naturally with virtually every mixer available.

Melon: Soft green, exudes freshness. Refreshing and mouthwatering honeydew melon. Simple yet complex. Smooth on the palate, serve on the rocks, or use to create summertime cocktails.

Oyzo – Akropolis: The traditional spirit aperitif of Greece. The distinctive flavour is derived from the seed of the anise plant. A neutral grain spirit flavoured with anise and distilled in New Zealand.

Peach: The flavour of fresh peaches and natural peach juice make this cocktail lover's dream.

Peachtree Schnapps: Crystal clear, light liqueur, bursting with the taste of ripe peaches. Drink chilled or on the rocks or mix with any soft drink or juice.

Rum – Bacardi: A smooth, dry, light bodied rum, especially suited for drinks in which you require subtle aroma and delicate flavour.

Rum – Captain Morgan: Its full flavour and bouquet make it ideal for mixing with juices and splits.

Rye Whisky – Canadian Club: The largest selling Canadian Whiskey in North America and Australia. Distilled from corn, rye and malted barley. A light, mild and delicate Whisky, ideal for drinking straight or in mixed cocktails.

Sabra: A unique flavour which comes from tangy jaffa oranges, with a hint of chocolate.

Sambuca – Black: Perfect after dinner or as an aperitif. The delicate oil from the Elderbush. The rich flavour of anise, with the subtle essence of lemon. Mingled, they are the dark secret of black sambuca's delightful flavour.

Sambuca – Clear: Made from elderberries with a touch of anise.

Scotch Whisky – Chives Regal: No. 1 Premium Scotch Whisky in the world. Aged for a minimum of 12 years. Fullest rich fruity taste, moreish, breadth of flavour.

Scotch Whisky – The Black Douglas: Australia's favourite Scotch Whisky. Distilled and blended in Scotland, and bottled in Australia. A soft, well-aged product that has a smooth finish.

Scotch Whisky – The Glenlivet: One of the top three Pure Single Malt in the world, aged for a minimum of 12 years. Delicate balance between sweetness and malty dryness.

Southern Comfort: A liqueur not a bourbon as often thought. It is unique, full-bodied liquor with a touch of sweetness. Its recipe is a secret, but it is known to be based on peaches and apricots. It is the largest selling liqueur in Australia.

Strawberry: Fluorescent red, unmistakable strawberry bouquet. Natural liqueur delivers a true to nature, fresh strawberry flavour.

Tennessee Whiskey – Jack Daniel's: Contrary to popular belief, Jack Daniel's is not a bourbon, it is a distinctive product called Tennessee Whiskey. Made from the 'old sour mash' process. Leached through hard maple charcoal, then aged in charred white oak barrels, at a controlled temperature, acquiring its body, bouquet and colour, yet remaining smooth.

Tequila – Coyote: Made to an old Mexican recipe in the town of Tequila, Jalisco, Mexico. A clear tequila made from the agave plant; it has a scented clean character and a slight burn. Perfect for drinking straight with salt and lemon, or as a great mixer.

Tia Maria: A liqueur with a cane spirit base, and its flavour derived from the finest Jamaican coffee. It is not too sweet with a subtle taste of coffee.

Vermouth: By description, Vermouth is a herbally infused wine. Three styles are most prevalent, these are:

> **Rosso:** A bitter sweet herbal flavour, often drunk as an aperitif.
> **Bianco:** Is light, fruity and refreshing. Mixes well with soda, lemonade and fruit juices.
> **Dry:** Is crisp, light and dry and is used as a base for many cocktails.

Vodka – ABSOLUT: The sixth largest selling spirit in the world. Its special distillation process ensures the highest quality premium vodka. ABSOLUT VODKA has the perfect balance of purity and a smooth bready, malty taste and aroma.

After Eight

Ingredients
Glass: Cordial (Embassy)
Mixers: 10ml Seagram's Creme de Cafe Liqueur
             10ml Seagram's Creme de Menthe Liqueur
             20ml Baileys Irish Cream
             15ml Southern Comfort

Method
Pour in order.
Technique: Shoot.
Comments: A peppermint surprise.

Atomic Bomb

Ingredients
Glass: Tall Dutch Cordial
Mixers: 20ml Tia Maria
             15ml Seagram's London Dry Gin
             10ml Cream

Method
Layer in order, then float cream.
Technique: Shoot.
Comments: A strategic 'one shooter weapon', this drink explodes down the unsuspecting throat. Delicious in emergencies! Gin may be replaced with Cointreau, or Seagram's Triple Sec.

B & B Shooter

Ingredients
Glass: Cordial (Lexington)
Mixers: 18ml Martell Cognac or Chatelle Napoleon
Brandy
18ml DOM Benedictine

Method
Pour in order.

Technique: Shoot.

Comments: For mature drinkers! Grandpa can turn up the pace of his medication. The Shooter is quick and smooth, the traditional B & B cocktail is normally served in a brandy balloon.

Banana Split

Ingredients
Glass: Tall Dutch Cordial
Mixers: 15ml Seagram's Creme de Cafe Liqueur
15ml Seagram's Banana Liqueur
10ml Seagram's Strawberry Liqueur
Whipped Cream

Method
Layer in order and top with whipped cream.

Technique: Shoot.

Comments: Let this one slip down sweetly, with a super strawberry aftertaste.

Bee Sting

Ingredients

Glass: Cordial (Embassy)
Mixers: 20ml Coyote Tequila
10ml Yellow Chartreuse

Method

Layer in order, then light.
Technique: Straw shoot while flaming.
Comments: Ouch! The Yellow Chartreuse attacks your throat with a numbing, pleasurable pain, as Tequila buzzes you back to the party. Drink quickly so the straw won't melt!

Black Nuts

Ingredients

Glass: Cordial (Embassy)
Mixers: 15ml Black Sambuca
15ml Frangelico

Method

Layer in order.
Technique: Shoot.
Comments: A wonderful "nutty" flavour, with a real anise touch.

Black Widow

Ingredients

Glass: Cordial (Embassy)
Mixers: 10ml Seagram's Strawberry Liqueur
10ml Black Sambuca
10ml Cream

Method

Layer in order.

Technique: Shoot.

Comments: Watch this one, the spider will get you quickly.

Blood Bath

Ingredients

Glass: Whisky Shot
Mixers: 10ml Cinzano Rosso Vermouth
15ml Seagram's Strawberry Liqueur
20ml Coyote Tequila

Method

Pour in order then layer the Tequila.

Technique: Shoot.

Comments: Cherry grins and rosy cheeks characterise the after effects of this blood thirsty experience. Only issued after midnight and before dawn.

Blow Job

Ingredients
Glass: Cordial (Lexington)
Mixers: 25ml Seagram's Creme de Menthe Liqueur
              12ml Baileys Irish Cream

Method
Layer in order and shoot.
Technique: Shoot.
Comments: A light minty confectionery flavour and creamy texture provide a mouthful for those who indulge. Twist this to a **"Rattlesnake"** by adding Green Chartreuse.

Brain Damage

Ingredients
Glass: Cordial (Lexington)
Mixers: 22ml Seagram's Coconut Liqueur
              10ml Seagram's Parfait Amour Liqueur
              5ml Seagram's Advocaat Liqueur

Method
Layer the Parfait Amour and Coconut Liqueur, then pour the Advocaat.
Technique: Shoot.
Comments: Separation induces restless nights, Advocaat intervenes to mould the senses.

Brave Bull

Ingredients
Glass: Whisky Shot
Mixers: 30ml Seagram's Creme de Cafe Liqueur
           15ml Coyote Tequila

Method
Layer in order.
Technique: Shoot.
Comments: One of my favourites for late night revellers, will resist fatigue and maintain stamina. Add Akropolis Ouzo and a **"TKO"** is punched out.

Candy Cane

Ingredients
Glass: Tall Dutch Cordial
Mixers: 15ml Seagram's Grenadine Cordial
           15ml Seagram's Creme de Menthe Liqueur
           25ml ABSOLUT VODKA

Method
Layer in order and shoot.
Technique: Shoot.
Comments: A real candy flavour, with a touch of menthol.

Chastity Belt

Ingredients

Glass: Tall Dutch Cordial
Mixers: 20ml Tia Maria
10ml Frangelico Hazelnut Liqueur
10ml Baileys Irish Cream
5ml Cream

Method

Layer in order, then float the cream.
Technique: Shoot.
Comments: Morality implores you not to succumb to the super-sweet delicacies of drinking's perversity.

Chilli Shot

Ingredients

Glass: Whisky Shot
Mixers: 45ml ABSOLUT VODKA
Slice of red chilli pepper

Method

Pour.
Technique: Shoot.
Comments: Feeling mischievous? Refrigerate the ABSOLUT VODKA with one red chilli pepper (or 3 to 5 drops of Tabasco sauce) for 24 hours before serving.

Chocolate Nougat

Ingredients
Glass: Cordial (Lexington)
Mixers: 10ml Frangelico Hazelnut Liqueur
10ml DOM Benedictine
10ml Baileys Irish Cream

Method
Pour in order then layer the Baileys Irish Cream.
Technique: Shoot.
Comments: *A swirling pleasure zone of flowing Baileys Irish Cream, above the finest Benedictine and based with voluptuous hazelnuts, accentuating the meaning of chocolate.*

Coathanger

Ingredients
Glass: Cordial (Lexington)
Mixers: 15ml Cointreau*
15ml Coyote Tequila
7ml Seagram's Grenadine Cordial
Drop of milk

Method
Layer Coyote Tequila onto the Cointreau, dash Cordial or Grenadine then drop the milk.
Technique: Shoot, then cup hand entirely over the rim, insert straw between fingers into the glass and inhale fumes.
Comments: *A euphoric experience, quiet stunning to your senses.*
Cointreau may be replaced with Seagram's Triple Sec Liqueur.

Courting Penelope

Ingredients

Glass: Cordial (Lexington)
Mixers: 22ml Martell Cognac
        15ml Grand Marnier

Method

Pour in order.
Technique: Shoot.
Comments: A distinctive acquired taste is needed for two inseparable moments!

Dark Sunset

Ingredients

Glass: Tall Dutch Cordial
Mixers: 22ml Seagram's Dark Creme de Cacao
        Liqueur
        22ml Malibu

Method

Layer in order.
Technique: Shoot.
Comments: This tropical paradise reflects sunset, beaches and the ripe coconuts of Malibu.

Devil's Handbrake

Ingredients

Glass: Tall Dutch Cordial
Mixers: 15ml Seagram's Banana Liqueur
15ml Mango Liqueur
15ml Seagram's Cherry Brandy Liqueur

Method

Layer in order.

Technique: Shoot.

Comments: A magnificent bounty off fruit infiltrated by the devil. Exquisite after a swim

Dirty Orgasm

Ingredients

Glass: Tall Dutch Cordial
Mixers: 15ml Seagram's Triple Sec Liqueur
15ml Galliano
15ml Baileys Irish Cream

Method

Layer in order.

Technique: Shoot.

Comments: The Irish frolic between the world's two best lovers, Italian Galliano and French Cointreau. Also known as a "**Screaming Orgasm**". Drambuie may replace Galliano.

Double Date

Ingredients
Glass: Tall Dutch Cordial
Mixers: 15ml Seagram's Melon Liqueur
             15ml White Creme de Menthe
             15ml DOM Benedictine

Method
Layer in order.
Technique: Tandem.
Comments: Soothing Creme de Menthe restrains the passion of DOM and Melon. For romantics.

Face Off

Ingredients
Glass: Tall Dutch Cordial
Mixers: 10ml Seagram's Grenadine Cordial
             10ml Seagram's Creme de Menthe Liqueur
             10ml Seagram's Parfait Amour Liqueur
             10ml Sambuca

Method
Layer in order.
Technique: Shoot.
Comments: Too many of these will certainly cause a loss of face.

Fizzy Rush

Ingredients

Glass: Tall Dutch Cordial
Mixers: 5ml White Creme de Menthe
10ml Apricot Brandy
30ml Champagne

Method

Pour in order.

Technique: Shoot.

Comments: Bubbles of refreshing Apricot guaranteed to get up your nose.

Flaming Lamborghini Shooter

Ingredients

Glass: Cordial (Embassy)
Mixers: 10ml Seagram's Creme de Cafe Liqueur
10ml Galliano
10ml Green Chartreuse

Method

Layer in order, then light.

Technique: Shoot while flaming.

Comments: Get the party into motion. Essential for birthday celebrants.

Flaming Lover

Ingredients

Glass: Cordial (Embassy)
Mixers: 15ml Sambuca
15ml Seagram's Triple Sec Liqueur

Method

Pour Triple Sec over lit Sambuca while drinking through a straw.

Technique: Straw shoot while flaming.

Comments: The Triple Sec softens the flame for inexperienced drinkers of flaming shooters.

Flaming Orgy

Ingredients

Glass: Tall Dutch Cordial
Mixers: 10ml Seagram's Grenadine Cordial
10ml Seagram's Creme de Menthe Liqueur
15ml Chatelle Napoleon Brandy
10ml Coyote Tequila

Method

Technique: Straw shoot while flaming.

Comments: Another of the potent flaming shooters. Don't get your lips too close to this one.

Flaming Sambuca

Ingredients

Glass: Cordial (Embassy)
Mixers: 30ml Sambuca
3 Coffee Beans

Method

Pour Sambuca, float coffee beans and light.

Technique: Shoot after flame extinguished.

Comments: Provides relief from the cold winter. The other way we do it, is to pour Sambuca into a wine glass then light. Cup your hand entirely over the rim while it flames, creating suction. Shake the glass, place under your nose, take your hand from the glass to inhale the fumes, then shoot!

Freddie Fud Pucker

Ingredients

Glass: Cordial (Lexington)
Mixers: 22ml Galliano
10ml Coyote Tequila
5ml Seagram's Orange Curacao Liqueur

Method

Layer Coyote Tequila onto Galliano then drop Orange Curacao.

Technique: Shoot.

Comments: Known to induce dancing on bars and at beach parties, be sure to mind your 'p's and 'f's when ordering.

Fruit Tingle

Ingredients
Glass: Cordial (Embassy)
Mixers: 10ml Seagram's Blue Curacao Liqueur
             15ml Mango Liqueur
             5ml Lemon juice

Method
Layer in order, optional to stir.
Technique: Shoot.
Comments: Tangy and piquant. Seagram's Melon Liqueur may be substituted for Mango Liqueur.

Galliano Hot Shot

Ingredients
Glass: Galliano Shot Glass
Mixers: 15ml Galliano
             25ml Black Coffee
             5ml Cream

Method
Top Galliano with black coffee, then float cream.
Technique: Shoot.
Comments: When in a hurry, a great way to enjoy a liqueur coffee.

Golden Cadillac Shooter

Ingredients

Glass: Tall Dutch Cordial
Mixers: 15ml Seagram's White Creme de Cacao
Liqueur
20ml Galliano
10ml Cream

Method

Layer Galliano and White Creme de Cacao, then float cream.

Technique: Shoot.

Comments: Comfort in style is what the distilled cocoa beams give golden Galliano – a real dazzler! The traditional Golden Cadillac cocktail has a larger volume, is shaken over ice and served in a 140ml Champagne Saucer.

Grand Slam

Ingredients

Glass: Cordial (Embassy)
Mixers: 10ml Seagram's Banana Liqueur
10ml Baileys Irish Cream
10ml Grand Marnier

Method

Pour in order.

Technique: Shoot.

Comments: Go for it!

Green Slime

Ingredients

Glass: Whisky Shot
Mixers: 20ml Seagram's Melon Liqueur
             15ml ABSOLUT VODKA
             5ml Egg White

Method

Pour in order, then stir.
Technique: Shoot.
Comments: Add more egg white for greater slime. Melon will keep the taste buds occupied, Vodka dilutes the egg white.

Half Nelson

Ingredients

Glass: Whisky Shot
Mixers: 15ml Seagram's Creme de Menthe Liqueur
             10ml Seagram's Strawberry Liqueur
             20ml Grand Marnier

Method

Layer in order.
Technique: Shoot.
Comments: The referee is unable to break the grip of Strawberry locking its green opponent into an immovable position. For the temporarily incapacitated.

Harbour Lights

Ingredients
Glass: Cordial (Lexington)
Mixers: 12ml Seagram's Creme de Cafe Liqueur
                     12ml Sambuca
                     12ml Green Chartreuse

Method
Layer in order.
Technique: Straw shoot.
Comments: Glittering reflections sparkle on the harbour beside a candlelight dinner. Substitute Yellow Chartreuse if preferred.

Hard On

Ingredients
Glass: Tall Dutch Cordial
Mixers: 20ml Seagram's Creme de Cafe Liqueur
                     15ml Seagram's Banana Liqueur
                     10ml Cream

Method
Layer Seagram's Banana Liqueur onto Kahlúa, then float the cream.
Technique: Shoot.
Comments: The first to float cream, voted the most popular shooter.

Hellraiser

Ingredients

Glass: Whisky Shot
Mixers: 15ml Seagram's Melon Liqueur
                15ml Seagram's Strawberry Liqueur
                15ml Black Sambuca

Method

Layer in order.
Technique: Shoot.
Comments: *A hell of a drink!*

High And Dry

Ingredients

Glass: Cordial (Embassy)
Mixers: 10ml Cinzano Bianco Vermouth
                15ml Coyote Tequila
                5ml Cinzano Dry Vermouth

Method

Pour in order, then stir.
Technique: Shoot.
Comments: *Disguise the mischief of Coyote Tequila with Cinzano Dry Vermouth. Best served chilled.*

Inkahlúarable

Ingredients
Glass: Cordial (Embassy)
Mixers: 10ml Kahlúa
             10ml Seagram's Triple Sec Liqueur
             10ml Grand Marnier

Method
Layer in order.
Technique: Shoot.
Comments: Terminal illness can be momentarily postponed with this Kahlúa-based antidote.

Irish Flag

Ingredients
Glass: Cordial (Lexington)
Mixers: 12ml Seagram's Creme de Menthe Liqueur
             12ml Baileys Irish Cream
             12ml Chatelle Napoleon Brandy

Method
Layer in order.
Technique: Shoot.
Comments: A stroll through verdant pastures. Brandy may be replaced with Tullamore Dew-an Old Irish Whisky.

Italian Stallion

Ingredients

Glass: Cordial (Lexington)
Mixers: 15ml Seagram's Banana Liqueur
                     15ml Galliano
                     7ml Cream

Method

Pour Galliano onto Seagram's Banana Liqueur, then float cream. Optional to stir.

Technique: Shoot.

Comments: This creamy banana ride you won't forget.

Japanese Slipper

Ingredients

Glass: Tall Dutch Cordial
Mixers: 20ml Seagram's Melon Liqueur
                     15ml Seagram's Triple Sec Liqueur*
                     10ml Lemon juice

Method

Layer Triple Sec onto the Melon then float the Lemon juice. Optional to Stir.

Technique: Shoot.

Comments: Elegant and refreshing. Precision is required with measurements. To revive failing confidence and replenish that special feeling.

*Cointreau may be substituted for Triple Sec.

Jawbreaker

Ingredients

Glass: Whisky shot
Mixers: 45ml Apricot Brandy
              4-5 drops Tabasco Sauce

Method

Pour Apricot Brandy then drop Tabasco Sauce.
Technique: Shoot.
Comments: Grit your teeth after this shot, then slowly open your mouth.

Jellyfish

Ingredients

Glass: Cordial (Lexington)
Mixers: 10ml Blue Curacao Liqueur
              10ml Romana Sambuca
              10ml Baileys Irish Cream
              2 dashes of Grenadine

Method

Layer in order and pour Grenadine.
Technique: Shoot.
Comments: Watch out for sting at the end of this slippery shooter.

Jumping Jack Flash

Ingredients
Glass: Whisky Shot
Mixers: 15ml Tia Maria
15ml Captain Morgan Rum
15ml Jack Daniel's

Method
Layer in order.
Technique: Shoot.
Comments: Thrill seeking Jack Daniel's and his accomplices await this opportunity to shudder your soul.

Jumping Mexican

Ingredients
Glass: Whisky Shot
Mixers: 22ml Seagram's Creme de Cafe Liqueur
22ml Cougar Bourbon

Method
Layer in order.
Technique: Shoot.
Comments: Jump into Mexico's favourite pastime and bounce back into the party. For those keen on the Mexican Hat Dance.

Kamikaze Shooter

Ingredients
Glass: Whisky Shot
Mixers: 20ml ABSOLUT VODKA
15ml Cointreau*
10ml Lemon Juice

Method
Layer the Cointreau onto Vodka, float the lemon juice, then optional to stir.
Technique: Shoot.
Comments: Maintain freshness for large volumes by adding strained egg white. Mix in a jug and keep refrigerated. The traditional Kamikaze cocktail has the addition of Lime cordial, it is shaken over ice, strained and then served in a 140ml Cocktail Glass.
*Seagram's Triple Sec may be substituted for Cointreau.

K.G.B. Shooter

Ingredients
Glass: Cordial (Lexington)
Mixers: 12ml Kahlúa
12ml Grand Marnier
12ml Baileys Irish Cream

Method
Layer in order.
Technique: Shoot.
Comments: Grand Marnier adds an orange twist to the Kahlúa and Baileys Irish Cream. The traditional K.G.B. cocktail is built over ice with greater volume of ingredient. It is normally served in a 140ml Old Fashioned Spirit Glass.

Kool Aid

Ingredients

Glass: Cordial (Lexington)
Mixers: 10ml Seagram's Melon Liqueur
15ml Amaretto di Saronno
12ml ABSOLUT VODKA

Method

Layer in order.
Technique: Shoot.
Comments: A familiar mix with various names. Amaretto's caramel lacing prevents overheating.

Lady Throat Killer

Ingredients

Glass: Tall Dutch Cordial
Mixers: 20ml Seagram's Creme de Cafe Liqueur
15ml Seagram's Melon Liqueur
10ml Frangelico Hazelnut Liqueur

Method

Layer in order.
Technique: Shoot.
Comments: This superb mixture offers an exquisite after-taste. One of my favourite Shooters.

Lambada

Ingredients

Glass: Whisky Shot
Mixers: 15ml Mango Liqueur
                15ml Black Sambuca
                15ml Coyote Tequila

Method

Layer in order.
Technique: Shoot.
Comments: Wiggle your way to the bar and order the latest liqueur, Black Sambuca. Both the dance and the Shooter will excite your partner.

Laser Beam

Ingredients

Glass: Tall Dutch Cordial
Mixers: 22ml Seagram's Creme de Cafe Liqueur
                15ml Galliano

Method

Layer in order.
Technique: Shoot.
Comments: Your palate is illuminated on this celestial journey!

33

Lick Sip Suck

Ingredients

Glass: Whisky Shot
Mixers: 30ml Coyote Tequila
Lemon in quarters or slices
Salt

Method

Pour.

Technique: On the flat piece of skin between the base of your thumb and index finger, place a pinch of salt. Place a quarter of the lemon by you on the bar. Lick the salt off your hand, shoot the Tequila and then suck the lemon.

Comments: This famous method yields the utmost enjoyment from Tequila. Delicious!

Marc's Rainbow

Ingredients

Glass: Whisky Shot
Mixers: 7ml Seagram's Creme de Cafe Liqueur
8ml Seagram's Melon Liqueur
8ml Malibu
7ml Seagram's Banana Liqueur
8ml Galliano
7ml Grand Marnier

Method

Layer in order.

Technique: Shoot.

Comments: One of Melbourne's best shooter recipes. Discover the pot of gold at the end of the rainbow.

Margarita Shooter

Ingredients
Glass: Whisky Shot
Mixers: 15ml Cointreau*
15ml Coyote Tequila
10ml Lemon juice
5ml Lime juice

Method
Layer Coyote Tequila onto Cointreau, float lemon juice then dash the lime juice.
Technique: Shoot.
Comments: Everyone should take this plunge. Lemon and Lime neutralise the acid. This Shooter is similar to the traditional Margarita cocktail, which is of greater volume, shaken over ice and served in a salt rimmed Champagne Saucer.

*Seagram's Triple Sec may be substituted for Cointreau

Martian Hard On

Ingredients
Glass: Tall Dutch Cordial
Mixers: 15ml Seagram's Dark Creme de Cacao
15ml Seagram's Melon Liqueur
15ml Baileys Irish Cream

Method
Layer in order.
Technique: Shoot.
Comments: When you are a little green about the facts of life.

Melon Splice

Ingredients

Glass: Tall Dutch Cordial
Mixers: 15ml Seagram's Melon Liqueur
               15ml Galliano
               15ml Seagram's Coconut Liqueur

Method

Layer in order.
Technique: Shoot.
Comments: Synonymous with Sunday strolls and ice-cream. Flakes of ice may be sprinkled to chill.

Mexican Flag

Ingredients

Glass: Tall Dutch Cordial
Mixers: 15ml Seagram's Grenadine Cordial
               15ml Seagram's Creme de Menthe Liqueur
               15ml Coyote Tequila

Method

Layer in order and shoot.
Technique: Shoot.
Comments: Try this "South of the Border" flag waver.

Nude Bomb

Ingredients
Glass: Cordial (Embassy)
Mixers: 10ml Seagram's Creme de Cafe Liqueur
10ml Seagram's Banana Liqueur
10ml Amaretto di Saronno

Method
Layer in order.
Technique: Shoot.
Comments: Especially created for toga-parties and skinny-dipping.

Orgasm Shooter

Ingredients
Glass: Whisky Shot
Mixers: 22ml Cointreau*
22ml Baileys Irish Cream

Method
Layer in order.
Technique: Shoot.
Comments: After the first one, you most certainly will want another. The Shooter method is different to the traditional Orgasm cocktail, which is a longer drink, built over ice and served in a 210ml Old Fashioned Spirit Glass.
*Seagram's Triple Sec may be substituted for Cointreau.

Oyster Shooter

Ingredients

Glass: Cordial (Embassy)
Mixers: 10ml ABSOLUT VODKA
10ml Tomato juice
5ml Cocktail sauce (recipe page 10)
Worcestershire sauce to taste
Tabasco sauce to taste
1 Fresh oyster

Method

Pour tomato juice onto the ABSOLUT VODKA, float the cocktail sauce, dash sauces to taste and drop in oyster.
Technique: Shoot.
Comments: An early morning wake-up call, replenishing energy lost the night before. Also referred to as a Heart Starter.

Passion Juice

Ingredients

Glass: Whisky Shot
Mixers: 20ml Seagram's Orange Curacao Liqueur
10ml Seagram's Cherry Brandy Liqueur
15ml freshly squeezed Orange or Lemon juice

Method

Layer in order. Optional to stir.
Technique: Shoot.
Comments: A bitter sweet lift by garnishing liqueur passion with juices.

Peach Tree Bay

Ingredients
Glass: Tall Dutch Cordial
Mixers: 25ml Peachtree Schnapps
15ml Pimm's No. I Cup
5ml Seagram's Creme de Menthe Liqueur

Method
Layer the Pimm's onto the Peachtree Schnapps, then drop Green Creme de Menthe.
Technique: Shoot.
Comments: Conjuring an image of uninhabited places, cool refreshing Pimm's is minted with Green Creme de Menthe.

Peachy Bum

Ingredients
Glass: Tall Dutch Cordial
Mixers: 20ml Mango Liqueur
15ml Peachtree Schnapps
10ml Cream

Method
Layer in order.
Technique: Shoot.
Comments: Delightfully enriched and mellowed by fresh cream.

Pearl Necklace

Ingredients
Glass:　　Cordial (Embassy)
Mixers:　　15ml Seagram's Melon Liqueur
　　　　　　　15ml Pimm's No. I Cup

Method
Layer in order.
Technique: Shoot.
Comments: A dash of lemonade dilutes the zappy after-taste.

Perfect Match

Ingredients
Glass:　　Cordial (Lexington)
Mixers:　　18ml Seagram's Parfait Amour Liqueur
　　　　　　　18ml Malibu

Method
Layer in order.
Technique: Shoot.
Comments: Parfaits (Perfect), Amour (Love), proposes future happiness and togetherness under Malibu's exotic veil.

Pipeline

Ingredients
Glass: Cordial (Embassy)
Mixers: 15ml Coyote Tequila
             15ml Karloff Vodka

Method
Layer in order.
Technique: *Shoot.*
Comments: *Ride the wild surf in this pipeline.*

Pipsqueak

Ingredients
Glass: Cordial (Embassy)
Mixers: 20ml Frangelico Hazelnut Liqueur
             10ml ABSOLUT VODKA
             7ml Lemon juice

Method
Layer in order, then stir.
Technique: *Shoot.*
Comments: *Another favourite of mine. A quaint appetiser before dinner.*

Rabbit-Punch

Ingredients
Glass: Whisky Shot
Mixers: 10ml Campari
              10ml Seagram's Dark Creme de Cacao
              10ml Malibu
              15ml Baileys Irish Cream

Method
Pour in order then layer Baileys Irish Cream.
Technique: Shoot.
Comments: Baileys Irish Cream assures credibility and its softness will subtly inflict a powerful jab to wake you up and keep you on the hop!

Ready, Set, Go!

Ingredients
Glass: Tall Dutch Cordial
Mixers: 15ml Seagram's Strawberry Liqueur
              15ml Seagram's Banana Liqueur
              15ml Seagram's Melon Liqueur

Method
Layer in order.
Technique: Suction Straw-shoot.
Comments: Similar to a Traffic Light, with added sweetness – almost a fermented fruit salad.

Red Indian

Ingredients

Glass: Cordial (Lexington)
Mixers: 10ml Seagram's Dark Creme de Cacao
12ml Peachtree Schnapps
15ml Canadian Club

Method

Layer in order.
Technique: Shoot.
Comments: Dark Creme de Cacao ripens the Peachtree to tantalise. CC takes the scalp!

Rusty Nail

Ingredients

Glass: Cordial (Embassy)
Mixers: 15ml The Black Douglas Scotch Whisky
15ml Drambuie

Method

Layer in order.
Technique: Shoot.
Comments: A pillow-softener, though this age-old blend will never cause fatigue. As a Shooter, great as "one for the road". The traditional cocktail is normally built over ice, in a 210ml Old Fashioned Spirit Glass.

Ryan's Rush

Ingredients

Glass: Cordial (Embassy)
Mixers: 10ml Seagram's Creme de Cafe Liqueur
10ml Baileys Irish Cream
10ml Bacardi

Method

Layer in order.

Technique: Shoot.

Comments: An easy one. Don't be lulled by the pleasant taste, this one has a real kick.

Screaming Death Shooter

Ingredients

Glass: Tall Dutch Cordial
Mixers: 15ml Seagram's Creme de Cafe Liqueur
10ml Cougar Bourbon
10ml DOM Benedictine
5ml Jack Daniel's
5ml Bundaberg OP

Method

Layer in the above order. Lighting optional.

Technique: Shoot while flaming.

Comments: The pinnacle of endurance. Double layers of flammable fuel cushioned in ascending order by Kahlúa, Bourbon and Benedictine, which sweetly numbs any pain. It's truth and dare.

Screwdriver Shooter

Ingredients
Glass: Whisky Shot
Mixers: 15ml Seagram's Orange Curacao Liqueur
                     30ml ABSOLUT VODKA

Method
Layer in order.

Technique: Shoot.

Comments: Add a dash of Peachtree Schnapps and it's known as a **"Fuzzy Navel"**. The Shooter mix departs from the traditional Screwdriver cocktail by the substitution of Orange Curacao for Orange Juice. The cocktail is also built over ice in a 210ml Old Fashioned Spirit Glass.

Sex In The Snow

Ingredients
Glass: Cordial (Lexington)
Mixers: 12ml Seagram's Triple Sec Liqueur
                     12ml Malibu
                     12ml Akropolis Ouzo

Method
Pour in order, then stir.

Technique: Straw shoot.

Comments: The sub-zero temperature of this combination is chillingly refreshing when drunk through a straw.

Sherbert Burp

Ingredients
Glass: Tall Dutch Cordial
Mixers: 15ml Seagram's Strawberry Liqueur
                 30ml Mumm Cordon Rouge Champagne

Method
Pour Strawberry Liqueur then top up with Champagne.
Technique: Shoot.
Comments: Change the colour of your burp with any flavoured liqueur. Even better, multi-colour it!

Sidecar Shooter

Ingredients
Glass: Cordial (Lexington)
Mixers:-   12ml Chatelle Napoleon Brandy
                 15ml Cointreau*
                 10ml Lemon juice

Method
Layer Cointreau onto Brandy, float lemon juice, then optional to stir.
Technique: Shoot.
Comments: This old-fashioned, lemon-barley refreshment, filtered through Cointreau and lightly tanned with Brandy, restores your zest for life. A slightly different mix to the traditional Sidecar cocktail, which is shaken over ice and served in a 90ml Cocktail Glass.
*Cointreau may be substituted with Seagram's Triple Sec.

Silver Thread

Ingredients
Glass: Tall Dutch Cordial
Mixers: 15ml Seagram's Creme de Menthe Liqueur
15ml Seagram's Banana Liqueur
15ml Tia Maria

Method
Layer in order.
Technique: Shoot or lick, sip and suck.
Comments: A great shooter to mend the fences. Try this one on with the "oldies".

Slippery Nipple

Ingredients
Glass: Cordial (Embassy)
Mixers: 30ml Sambuca
15ml Baileys Irish Cream

Method
Layer in order.
Technique: Shoot.
Comments: One of the originals, very well received. Cream floated on the Baileys becomes a **"Pregnant Slippery Nipple".** Grand Marnier included makes a **"Slipadicthome"**.

Snake-Bite

Ingredients
Glass: Cordial (Embassy)
Mixers: 20ml Seagram's Creme de Cafe Liqueur
                10ml Green Chartreuse

Method
Layer in order, then light.
Technique: Straw shoot while flaming.
Comments: Score this shooter ten out of ten. Drink quickly or the straw will melt.

Spanish Fly

Ingredients
Glass: Whisky Shot
Mixers: 10ml Cinzano Bianco Vermouth
                15ml Coyote Tequila
                20ml The Black Douglas Scotch Whisky

Method
Technique: Tandem.
Comments: No, it's not what you're twinkling eye and devious smirk assumes...it's better. A guaranteed survival capsule, capable of producing fantasies beyond those Spain is famous for.

Springbok

Ingredients
Glass: Cordial (Embassy)
Mixers: 20ml Passionfruit Syrup
10ml Seagram's Creme de Menthe Liqueur
5ml Aphrodite Ouzo

Method
Layer in order.
Technique: Shoot.
Comments: Named after the beautiful springbok of Africa, formerly a motif on the South African Rugby jersey.

Strawberry Cream

Ingredients
Glass: Cordial (Embassy)
Mixers: 20ml Seagram's Strawberry Liqueur
10ml Cream

Method
Layer in order.
Technique: Shoot.
Comments: Begin your trip to the **"World of Shooters"** with this one. Cream acts as a buffer to entice the nervous and inexperienced. Strawberries calm what was needless concern.

Suction Cup

Ingredients

Glass: Cordial (Lexington)
Mixers: 20ml ABSOLUT VODKA
                  10ml Seagram's Melon Liqueur
                  7ml Seagram's Blue Curacao Liqueur

Method

Layer the Melon onto Vodka, then pour Blue Curacao.
Technique: Suction-straw shoot.
Comments: A supersonic vacuum results from this drinking method.

Suitor

Ingredients

Glass: Cordial (Lexington)
Mixers: 10ml Drambuie*
                  10ml Grand Marnier
                  10ml Baileys Irish Cream
                  7ml Milk

Method

Pour in order.
Technique: Shoot.
Comments: Milk inclusion coddles a cool moment, resettles anxieties when approaching the fair sex, guaranteed to excite romance.
*Drambuie may be substituted with Lochan Ora.

Sukiyaki

Ingredients
Glass: Cordial (Embassy)
Mixers: 10ml Mango Liqueur
10ml Apricot Brandy
10ml Malibu

Method
Layer in order.
Technique: Shoot.
Comments: Essential starter for a superb Japanese banquet.

Test Tube Baby

Ingredients
Glass: Tall Dutch Cordial
Mixers: 5ml White Creme de Menthe
10ml Apricot Brandy
30ml Champagne

Method
Pour in order.
Technique: Shoot.
Comments: Bubbles of refreshing Apricot guaranteed to get up your nose.

The Day After

Ingredients

Glass: Cordial (Embassy)
Mixers: 10ml Cointreau*
               10ml Coyote Tequila
               5 drops Seagram's Blue Curacao Liqueur
               10ml Green Chartreuse

Method

Layer Tequila onto Cointreau. Drop the Blue Curacao, then layer Green Chartreuse and light.

Technique: Shoot after flame extinguished.

Comments: An upside down day!

*Cointreau may be substituted with Seagram's Triple Sec.

T.K.O.

Ingredients

Glass: Cordial (Embassy)
Mixers: 10ml Seagram's Creme de Cafe
               10ml Coyote Tequila
               10ml Akropolis Oyzo

Method

Layer in order.

Technique: Shoot.

Comments: Don't fall with this TKO, drink it with pleasure, recover without pain.

Tickled Pink

Ingredients
Glass: Whisky Shot
Mixers: 40ml White Creme de Menthe Liqueur
5ml Seagram's Grenadine Cordial

Method
Pour White Creme de Menthe followed by a dash of Grenadine or Raspberry Cordial.
Technique: Shoot.
Comments: For those who are bashful when complimented.

Towering Inferno

Ingredients
Glass: Cordial (Embassy)
Mixers: 10ml Seagram's London Dry Gin
10ml Seagram's Triple Sec Liqueur
10ml Green Chartreuse

Method
Layer in order, then light.
Technique: Shoot while flaming.
Comments: Designed to set the night on fire.

Traffic Light

Ingredients

Glass: Tall Dutch Cordial
Mixers: 10ml Seagram's Strawberry Liqueur
10ml Galliano
25ml Green Chartreuse

Method

Layer in order, then light.
Technique: Suction-straw shoot.
Comments: Ready set go! Substitute Seagram's Banana Liqueur for Galliano and Seagram's Melon Liqueur for Green Chartreuse, for those with a sweet tooth.

U-Turn

Ingredients

Glass: Whisky Shot
Mixers: 15ml Seagram's Banana Liqueur
30ml Tia Maria

Method

Layer in order.
Technique: Shoot.
Comments: The Banana offers the curve yet its Tia Maria that sends you around the bend. A complete change of direction.

Vodka-Tini

Ingredients

Glass: Cordial (Embassy)
Mixers: 25ml ABSOLUT VODKA
5ml Cinzano Dry Vermouth

Method

Pour in order, then stir.
Technique: Shoot.
Comments: No olive is required. Preferably served chilled.

Water-Bubba

Ingredients

Glass: Cordial (Embassy)
Mixers: 15ml Seagram's Cherry Advocaat Liqueur
10ml Seagram's Advocaat Liqueur
12ml Seagram's Blue Curacao Liqueur

Method

Pour Advocaat into Cherry Advocaat, then layer the Blue Curacao.
Technique: Shoot.
Comments: The Advocaat resembles an egg yolk, with veins of Cherry Advocaat. Also known as an **"Unborn Baby"**.

Index